T0361300

A SILVER CASKET AND STRAINER
FROM THE WALBROOK MITHRAEUM
IN THE CITY OF LONDON

ÉTUDES PRÉLIMINAIRES
AUX RELIGIONS ORIENTALES
DANS L'EMPIRE ROMAIN

PUBLIÉES PAR

M. J. VERMASEREN

TOME QUATRIÈME

J. M. C. TOYNBEE

A SILVER CASKET AND STRAINER
FROM THE WALBROOK MITHRAEUM
IN THE CITY OF LONDON

LEIDEN
E. J. BRILL
1963

The Casket: General View.

J. M. C. TOYNBEE

A SILVER CASKET AND STRAINER FROM THE WALBROOK MITHRAEUM IN THE CITY OF LONDON

WITH A FRONTISPIECE AND 15 PLATES

LEIDEN
E. J. BRILL
1963

The silver casket and strainer which form the subject of this study came to light on 8 October 1954 in the Mithraeum excavated by Professor W. F. Grimes for the Roman and Mediaeval London Excavation Council in the autumn of that year at Walbrook in the City of London, and are now in the Guildhall Museum (shortly to form part of the Museum of London *). They were found on the top of what remained of the temple's north wall, towards its western end. But it would appear that above the place where the casket and strainer lay about 18 inches of ancient wall had been removed when a pit had been dug at that spot for nineteenth-century foundations [1]), so that originally these objects must have been inserted *in* the wall in Roman times, seemingly with a view to concealing them. The fact that close to the casket and strainer there were discovered fragments of a Roman silver bowl with late-looking punched decoration, presumably smashed by the modern building operations, when the casket and strainer themselves were mercifully missed by them, certainly suggests that all these pieces of precious metal belonged to a deliberately hidden *cache*—hidden possibly on the same occasion as that on which five fine sculptures of Italian marble, dating from the second century A.D., were buried in hollows under the temple floor probably at some date during the first half of the fourth century [2]). But that would, of course, be no proof that the casket and strainer were contemporary with the marbles.

I. The casket, which is circular (Frontispiece), is $2\frac{1}{2}$ inches (6.3 cm) high, 10 inches (25.4 cm) in circumference, $3\frac{1}{8}$ inches (8 cm) in outer, and 3 inches (7.5 cm) in inner, diameter. It carries a close-fitting, slightly convex, round lid, $3\frac{1}{10}$ inches (7.8 cm) in diameter

*) It is with Professor Grimes's kind permission that the following account of the casket and strainer, originally prepared for his forthcoming *Report* on the excavation, is published here.

1) *The Times* 13 December 1958.

2) J. M. C. Toynbee, *Art in Roman Britain*, ed. 2, 1963, pp. 2-3; 132-3, no. 20, pl. 31; 134-5, no. 24, pl. 28; 141-5, nos. 36-8, pls. 40, 42, 43.

and perfectly preserved, except for part of the thin strip of metal which linked the hinge of the lid with the casket's rounded wall.

(A) *The Lid*. Opposite the hinge is the slot for the pin that fastened down the lid; and the pin itself, the head of which takes the form of the head of an animal, probably a mastiff, is surviving. Round the lid's circumference runs a very narrow beaded edging; and the whole of its upper surface is covered with figure ornament, cast in relief and chased and revealing here and there traces of gilding (Pl. I).

These designs consist of small figures of men and animals, with a few landscape accessories, and they fall into seven clearly defined groups. (1) In the centre of the field, and orientated slightly off the axis of the hinge and pin, are the head and foreparts of an elephant, standing towards the right. Only its right foreleg is visible, while its hindlegs and hindquarters retreat into the background, out of which it seems to be emerging. With its trunk and right tusk the elephant is mauling the head of an apparently shaggy-coated animal, possibly a wild goat, which crouches on the ground towards the left. A ridge represents the ground-line below the elephant, but under the goat (?) this is not continued. (2) Immediately above the head of the elephant in (1), and facing towards the right, is a winged Griffin, the forelegs of which bestride a large, oblong, box-shaped object (PL. II). The Griffin appears to be attacking with its beak the right-hand end of this box. Near the rim of the lid, just to the right of the Griffin's head, a St. Andrew's cross is incised within a square. This mark, of which the purpose is obscure, bears no relation to the ornament. (3) To the right of (2) is a group of three human figures (Pl. III). Above, a man stands towards the right, bending down and with both arms extended in the direction of a sloping ledge of rock, from the right-hand end of which project two heavy boulders. He appears to be balancing himself upon the left-hand upper corner of another oblong box, similar to that in (2). But the top of its right-hand end is open; and through this aperture emerge towards the right the head and trunk of a second man. His arms are extended before him and his hands are grasped by those of a third man, facing to the left, with both knees bent as he lunges eagerly forward. This man is obviously pulling the second member of the trio out of the box-like object. (4) Opposite (3), on the left-hand side of (2), is another winged Griffin standing towards the left on a third oblong box, the end of which, as in (2), is closed (Pl. IV). Like its counterpart in (2), this creature is pecking vigorously at the top of the box, and its long tail curls up round the right hindfoot of the beast in (2), with which it is otherwise quite unconnected. (5) Below (4) is a leafless tree, the trunk of which curves to follow the line of the lid's circumference, while its branches spread inwards towards the centre of the field. At the end of the longest branch there perches what appears to be a very large bird, shown vertically, with its head reaching up beside the right-hand end of the box in (4) and its tail thrusting downwards between the tree-trunk and the elephant in (1). From the foot of the tree a ground-line runs out towards the right and supports an animal, probably a panther, the foreparts of which are seen creeping from behind the trunk, as it looks back furtively towards the left. Here, again, the hindquarters of the beast disappear into the background. (6) Below the foreleg of the elephant in (1) another animal, possibly a boar, is advancing towards the right. Only the legs in the foreground are rendered. A snake has twined itself round the creature's body and bites it in the neck. The details at this point are far from clear; and it is not easy to decide whether the boar's (?) snout is facing straight ahead or is turned sharply backwards to retaliate. (7) Finally, below the goat (?) in (1) a feline creature, most probably another panther, bounds towards the right over rocks (?). Its tail swings out behind, its head is turned three-quarters towards the left, and beneath its forepaws sprawls another animal, perhaps a deer, seen from behind, with its head towards the left, its body bent along the lid's curving line, and its tail flying up towards the rocks in (3). This completes the circle.

(B) *The Wall.* The exterior wall of the casket (Pl. VIII) is, like the upper surface of its lid, completely filled with figures of men and animals set in a landscape setting of trees and rocks. Here, again, the ornament was produced by casting in a mould, followed by chasing. The relief-work is bounded at top and bottom by a pair of convex mouldings, of which the upper one, encircling the lid, takes the form of a laurel-wreath, while the lower one, girdling the base, is incised with a row of 'tongues' projecting downwards. This frieze-like design is, in general effect, continuous all the way round the vessel. But it breaks up, on closer view, into four main scenes or episodes, the beginnings and ends of which are marked either by trees or rocks or by abrupt changes in the direction of the figures. The most strongly accented of these lines of demarcation is a tree which reaches right across the frieze, from bottom to top, a short distance to the spectator's left of the fastening-pin on the lid (near the right-hand end). This tree, which has a gnarled trunk and large, flat leaves, or open flowers, at the ends of its spreading branches, may be taken as intended by the artist to indicate the start and finish of the story; and our description may conveniently begin with the scene on its immediate right.

(1) The first scene (the right-hand end) is framed on one side by the tree just described and on the other by a barren tree-trunk reaching half-way up the frieze (the left-hand end). It is arranged, as are also the three other scenes, in two superimposed tiers or storeys. Above, on the left, a man strides towards the right along a ledge of rock, with his left leg advanced (Pl. V). He wears a conical helmet and probably a close-fitting jerkin and breeches; and at his waist swings a sheathed knife. Facing him and striding upon the roof of a rocky cave, is another man, probably also clad in a jerkin and breeches, but with a hood (?) instead of a helmet. His right leg is advanced and his left leg and left hand are concealed behind a large oblong contraption, which he seems to be dragging diagonally after him or out of which he is stepping. On its lower edge are two round blobs; and the only explanation of it that the present writer can offer is that this is a box, generally similar to, but of a somewhat different type from, those already described on the lid of the casket, of which we see one side with small wheels or casters attached to it. Above the box towers what looks like a pinnacle of rock or a branchless tree-trunk. The two men are joining right hands and are clearly not in combat, but are either greeting one another or conversing on some urgent matter. Just below their hands is a small round object, probably a stone. Beside the first man's right leg a small hole pierces the background. In the lower tier, on the left, a large, coiled snake rears itself up towards the right (Pl. VI). On the right,

facing the snake, there cowers at the entrance to the rocky cave a long-snouted, thick-set, short-legged, thin-tailed creature, not unlike a tapir, but probably meant to represent a mongoose. The rearing snake would seem to have terrorised this beast.

(2) The second scene is terminated on the right by a tree-stump below and by a chimney-like rock, or branchless tree-trunk, rising from a wall of boulders, above. The upper storey is divided from the lower by a ledge or ground-line. At the left end of the ledge a winged Griffin crouches towards the right (Pl. VII). Facing it, in the centre, is a rearing snake, seen against what is either a tree-trunk or a jagged spur of rock and, again, apparently opposed to the confronting Griffin; and on the right the Griffin is balanced by a feline—a tiger or a panther—standing, with waiving tail, towards the right, but looking back over its shoulder towards the snake. Below, from left to right, are (a) a man wearing a conical helmet, a jerkin or tunic, breeches(?), and a flying cloak, standing frontal, but looking to the right, with both arms stretched out before him; (b) a second man, similarly clad, striding towards the right, holding a small, oval shield on his left arm, while his right hand is raised to hurl a stone; (c) a third man, who has fallen on the ground, with his head towards the left and kicking legs and a large stone visible below his left foot; (d) the vertical body of a beast shown with its head downwards and its tail in air: this animal would seem to have overthrown the third man and to be the second man's target; (e) a hippopotamus standing unconcernedly towards the right, with a snake in its mouth and its back turned upon the scene of conflict, in front of the wall of boulders. Portions of the background are lost beneath the bellies of the Griffin and the feline in the upper tier, and there is a large perforation in the background below, extending from the second man to the middle of the hippopotamus.

(3) Here the tiers of figures are more closely related than in scenes (1) and (2). Above, on the left, a man is standing on a ledge with his legs set wide apart (Pl. IX). He wears a flat, round cap, a jerkin or tunic, breeches (?), and a cloak floating out like a sail towards the right. With his right hand he aims a stone at a lion, which occupies the right-hand portion of the lower tier and is rearing against the oval shield of a second man, shown immediately

below the first, wearing a flat, round cap and a jerkin, holding a long knife in his right hand, and being forced to the ground, with his right leg doubled up under him, by the impact of the animal. Below the belly of the lion lies a large stone that has missed its target. To the right of the first man, above the lion's head, is yet another oblong box, seen in perspective and seemingly open at one end. A narrow rectangular object, possibly the detachable door for closing the aperture, leans diagonally beside the box; and a gnarled tree with spreading branches, one of which ends in a large leaf or open flower, rounds off the scene.

(4) This section of the frieze is the longest of the four and consists entirely of animals, shown singly or in groups, ranged in two quite separate tiers, and interspersed with trees and rocks. The upper zone contains, from left to right:—(a) the foreparts of an elephant standing towards the right, with its hindquarters vanishing into the background, as in (1) on the lid, and a snake writhing over its back, and, again as in the lid scene, mauling with its tusks and trunk the head of another beast, here a panther-like creature, that crouches on the ground towards the left; (b) a tree, with large leaves, or open flowers, at the ends of its spreading branches; (c) a feline bounding towards the right over rocks (?); (d) another feline bounding towards the left, with a leafy tree in the background behind it; (e) a lion prancing towards the left and devouring an animal of indeterminate species. In the lower tier are seen, from left to right: —(a) a lion leaping towards the right over the body of a deer, which lies with its head towards the left; (b) possibly a bear, or more probably another hippopotamus, standing towards the right and mauling another beast that it has rolled upon its back; (c) a tree-stump; (d) a lion standing towards the left. The scene is bounded on the right by the large tree that forms the starting point; and there are perforations in the background to the right of the elephant, under the belly of the lion below the elephant, and beside the hind-quarters of the first feline in the upper tier.

Both on the lid and on the wall of the Walbrook casket the figures of men and animals are essentially three-dimensional, naturalistic, well proportioned, plastically modelled, and instinct with life and vigorous movement. Trees and rocks are, in general, conventionally treated, although the gnarled trunks of the trees between the first and fourth, and third and fourth, scenes are drawn with the realistic fidelity to Nature that marks the rendering of many of the animals. The individual figures and groups are, in fact, stylistically, as well as technically, in the full stream of Hellenistic art traditions, and they could, if taken in isolation, rank as the products of an early—to—mid—imperial workshop. But as compositions these designs, both on lid and wall, are completely lacking in organic coherence; and the effect is that of an 'all-over' carpet or tapestry pattern with loosely linked, self-contained units strewn across the field, with a view to covering every scrap of the surface with small-scale filling ornament. In this respect the casket's affinities are, as we shall see (pp. 9-11), less with the first and second centuries than with the late-antique as exemplified particularly on fourth- and fifth-century mosaic pavements; although much more organic 'all-over' designs had, of course, already appeared in the purely decorative 'free-style' wild beast scenes, with or without hunters, of the second-century 'samian' potters' repertory.

(C) *The Base.* On the under side of the very slightly convex base (Pl. X) are four lightly incised concentric circles, the two inner ones close together, the other two much more widely spaced. They were drawn with the compass, one point of which pierced a tiny hole in the metal at the centre. There is also a long perforation through the base on one side of this central point, between the third and fourth (outer) circles; and near this perforation is a faintly scratched *graffito* reading I S I Λ V I, probably a personal name in the genitive case, between the second and third circles [1]).

II. Inside the casket as found was a silver cylindrical strainer or filter (Pl. XI), not fitting it tightly, but conforming to it generally in shape and size and presumably intended for use with it. Within the strainer are three horizontal 'arms' springing from the wall just below the top and meeting at the centre; and on the outer surface of the wall can be seen the three rivets by which these 'arms' were held in place. The under side of the strainer's base is slightly convex;

1) *JRS*, LI, 1961, p. 195, no. 16.

and this base is perforated by a series of small holes that form an attractive and highly decorative geometric pattern (Pl. XIII). In the middle is an eight-petalled rosette, with a dot at its centre, a group of four dots on each petal, and an external dot continuing the line that divides each petal from its fellow. Outside the rosette is a circle of dots and then eight curving, scroll-like lines that combine to make a cushion-shaped square, with eight spirals curling alternately inwards and outwards and two groups of dots flanking each spiral. The whole is finally enclosed within another circle.

A close parallel to this strainer is afforded by a very slightly larger silver cylindrical strainer found at Stráže in Czecho-Slovakia, which has the same three internal 'arms', but with a knob at their point of junction, and perforations in the bottom that are set out in a series of simple concentric circles (Pl. XII) [1]). It was found in a grave and is dated to the third century A.D.

Assuming that the Walbrook casket served as a container in Mithraic ritual and that the strainer functioned with it, its contents must have been liquid. This liquid can hardly have been blood for smearing on initiates, since blood would have congealed and have been anyhow too thick to pass through the perforations in the base of the strainer. The filter might, on the other hand, have been used for straining honey into the casket. Porphyry tells us [2]) that those who were being initiated into the grade of *Leones* had honey instead of water poured over their hands for cleansing purposes (ὅταν μὲν οὖν τοῖς τὰ λεοντικὰ μυομένοις εἰς τὰς χεῖρας ἀνθ' ὕδατος μέλι νίψασθαι ἐγχέωσι) and that their tongues were purified by honey from every stain of sin (καθαίρουσι δὲ καὶ τὴν γλῶτταν τῷ μέλιτι ἀπὸ παντὸς ἁμαρτωλοῦ).

An alternative possibility is that the strainer was used for infusing a concoction of herbs which served to induce a ritual hypnosis in Mithraic (or some other) mystery-cult; that the triple 'arms' were to mark the limit of the amount of drug to be infused; and that

1) V. Ondrouch, *Bohaté Hroby z Doby Rímskej na Slovensku* (*Recent Finds from Roman Tombs in Slovakia*), 1957, p. 148, no. 10, fig. 34; p. 246; pl. 35, fig. 3. The present writer owes this reference to Mrs. A. Cavendish.

2) *De antro nympharum*, 15: F. Cumont, *Textes et monuments figurés relatifs aux mystères de Mithra*, II, 1896, p. 40.

this strainer or infuser was the really important ritual object, the casket being merely its container [1]). But why should such elaborate decoration have been lavished on a box that was only meant to hold an implement when out of use?

III. The figured scenes on the lid and walls of the Walbrook casket are, as we have seen, hunting scenes, with men, some of them armed with defensive shields and helmets, engaged in catching animals, and with animals pulling down and slaying other beasts. The landscape elements of trees and rocks suggest that these hunts are in the field, in some distant African or Asiatic land, rather than examples of those staged *venationes* and beast-fights which were among the most popular forms of spectacle in the arenas of the Roman world. It is, indeed, in the great hunt mosaics of the later Empire, of which the primary purpose was to portray the pursuit and capture of wild creatures for such *venationes* and displays in the city amphiteatres, that the casket reliefs are most closely paralleled, both in subject-matter and in style and composition; and of these late mosaics five are of outstanding interest in our present context. Hunting scenes and animal combats are only some of the many, heterogeneous themes spread across the field of the great fifth-century mosaic pavement that adorns the ambulatory of the peristyle of the Byzantine palace at Istanbul [2]). But the general effect of those unconnected, self-contained groups, somewhat haphazardly arranged in tiers (in this case, in three tiers) to form an 'all-over' design, is strikingly similar to that of the work now under discussion; and there, as here, the individual motifs have all the plasticity, liveliness, and naturalism that are the familiar hall-marks of Hellenistic and early-to-mid-imperial art. Precisely the same conflation of earlier naturalism and late-antique schemes of composition characterises three fifth-to-sixth-century hunt mosaics from Antioch-on-the-Orontes,

1) The present writer owes this suggestion to Mr. R. Merrifield of the Guidhall Museum.
2) G. Brett, W. J. Macaulay, R. B. K. Stevenson, *The Great Palace of the Byzantine Emperors*, 1947. For scenes of hunting and animal combats, see pls. 28, 33, 36-9, 41-5. This mosaic has been dated by some scholars to as late as the sixth century.

the Megalopsychia pavement in the 'Yakto Complex' [1]), the Dumbarton Oaks pavement [2]), and the pavement in the 'House of the Worcester Hunt'[3]).

It is, however, in the remarkable country villa recently made known near Piazza Armerina, in central Sicily, that we must turn for the most striking analogies to the relief work on our casket [4]). There, on the floor of an immense corridor, 70 yards (63.70 m.) long by 6 yards (5.46 m) wide and terminating in an apse at either end, is a truly amazing array of illustrations of the hunting, capturing, and transporting of wild beasts and birds for exhibition in the arena shows and *venationes*. This pavement tallies exactly with the casket scenes, first, in its many-tiered, 'all-over' patterning with separate episodes, related, indeed, in their general theme, but carelessly, sometimes even crudely, juxtaposed without any attempt to weld them into a single, unified picture [5]); secondly, in the verve, vivacity, and realism with which, in particular, its individual birds and animals are rendered. Furthermore, it is this Sicilian mosaic that provides us with counterparts of two of the most arresting items in the casket's repertory of motifs—the winged Griffins and the large, oblong, box-like objects.

Reference to Piazza Armerina leaves no room for doubt that the oblong objects are crates or cages, set by the hunters for catching the beasts and also used as travelling boxes for transporting them alive across the Mediterranean to the places of public entertainment

---

1) D. Levi, *Antioch Mosaic Pavements*, 1947, I, p. 324, fig. 136; II, pls. 77-8.

2) Levi, *o.c.*, I, pp. 358-9, fig. 148; II, pl. 86, a; G. M. A. Richter, *Catalogue of Greek and Roman Antiquities in the Dumbarton Oaks Collection*, 1956, pp. 62-3, no. 44, pl. 25, b.

3) Levi, *o.c.*, I, pp. 363-5, figs. 150-1; II, pl. 86, b.

4) From the considerable body of literature that Piazza Armerina has already inspired the following items may be cited here: G. V. Gentili (a) *La villa romana di Piazza Armerina* (*Itinerari dei Musei e Monumenti d'Italia*, No. 87) ed. 1, 1951; (b) *ibid.*, ed. 4, 1960; (c) *I mosaici della villa romana del casale di Piazza Armerina* in *BArte*, XXXVII (ser. 4, 1) 1952, pp. 33-46, figs. 1-20, pl. 1; (d) *La villa erculia di Piazza Armerina: i mosaici figurativi*, 1959; B. Pace, *I mosaici di Piazza Armerina*, 1955.

5) E.g. Gentili (a), figs. 16-20; Gentili (b), figs. 17-20; Gentili (c), pl. 1, b; Pace, *o.c.*, pl. 10, figs. 19, 22.

for which they were destined [1]). One such cage appears on wheels and drawn by oxen [2]); another is slung on a pole and carried along by a pair of huntsmen [3]); others, again, are ranged on board a cargo boat [4]). Moreover, the motif of a Griffin clambering over one of these boxes, shown twice on the lid of the Walbrook casket (scenes 2 and 4: pp. 2-3 and Pls. I, II and XIV), appears at the right-hand end of the mosaic, where a great winged Griffin, facing towards the left, sprawls on top of a slatted crate, out of the left-hand end of which there peeps a human face (Pl. XV) [5]). It would seem that men were sometimes immured in these boxes as baits; the quarry would sense their presence and try to tear the cages open in order to reach them, and then, while thus preoccupied, be the more easily taken captive by other hunters. Scene 3 on the casket lid represents the succeeding stage in such an episode: the human bait has served his turn and is being released from his confinement by two companions. That the Griffin was popularly, at least, believed to exist in the East as a creature that could be hunted is clear from Philostratus' *Life of Apollonius of Tyana* (iii, 48): —'For these animals (sc. οἱ γρῦπες) do exist in India and are held to be sacred to the Sun (τὰ γὰρ θηρία ταῦτα εἶναί τε ἐν Ἰνδοῖς καὶ ἱεροὺς νομίζεσθαι τοῦ Ἡλίου) . . . In size and strength they resemble lions, but having the advantage over them that they have wings, they will attack lions and get the better of elephants and dragons (μέγεθός τε καὶ ἀλκὴν εἰκάσθαι αὐτοὺς τοῖς λέουσιν, ὑπὸ δὲ πλεονεξίας τῶν πτερῶν αὐτοῖς τε ἐκείνοις ἐπιτίθεσθαι, καὶ τῶν ἐλεφάντων δὲ καὶ δρακόντων ὑπερτέρους εἶναι)'. There is, then, no need to read any particular mystic meaning into the Griffin. But under the Empire hunts and animal combats often carried more than their face-value significance when reproduced in a religious (as here) or funerary context, where they feature as allegories, partly of the fertility, and even of the pleasant pastimes, of the world beyond the grave

1) For such cages or boxes as traps, see J. Aymard, *Essai sur les chasses romaines*, 1951, pp. 450-5, pl. 3, a; 32.
2) Pace, *o.c.*, fig. 19; *cf.* Aymard, *o.c.*, pl. 7, a.
3) Gentili (c), p. 39, fig. 14.
4) Gentili (b), fig. 21; Gentili (c), p. 41, fig. 16; Gentili (d), pl. 25.
5) Gentili (a), fig. 16; Gentili (b), fig. 17.

and partly of the chasing and overpowering of the forces of wickedness by those of goodness.

Parallels in metal work to the style and some of the details of
the Walbrook casket are afforded by vessels in the fourth-century
silver treasure from Mildenhall in Suffolk [1]). On the great Oceanus
dish [2]), on the two Dionysiac platters [3]), on the hemispherical
cover [4]), and on the flanges of four bowls [5]) we are confronted with
human and animal figures that are as vivid, naturalistic, and springy
in movement as any on the London piece. The four last-mentioned
items also show, interspersed among the human heads and beasts
on their flanges, trees with spreading branches which terminate
in large, flat leaves, or open flowers, of the same type as those that
have been noted on the casket (pp. 4, 6) [6]). The technique of the
latter, with its scenes cast in relatively high relief, is, of course,
quite different from that of the Suffolk vessels, the ornament of
which, worked in very low relief, was produced by hammering down
the background from the front [7]). But other techniques, *repoussé*,
for example, were also employed in the late Roman period [8]);
and on every count the Walbrook casket would appear to be tho-
roughly at home in the *milieu* of the late-antique silver worker's
craft.

IV. The social and religious implications of the casket and the strainer, in the context in which they came to light, are less easy to define
than are those of the other works of art from the Walbrook Mithraeum, and the casket's date, judging by style alone, is, as we have
seen, not immediately obvious, while no deity or motif linking it

1) J. W. Brailsford, *The Mildenhall Treasure: a Handbook* (ed. 2), 1955.
2) *Ibid.*, pp. 5-6, no. 1, pl. 1.
3) *Ibid.*, pp. 6-7, nos. 2-3, pl. 2, a.
4) *Ibid.*, p. 9, no. 6, pl. 2, b.
5) *Ibid.*, pp. 9-11, nos. 7-10, pl. 4.
6) Similar trees appear in hunting scenes in a frieze on a Roman bronze
bucket found in Holland: M. H. P. den Boesterd, *Description of the Collections
in the Rijksmuseum G. M. Kam at Nijmegen*, v: *the Bronze Vessels*, 1956,
pp. 44-5, no. 146, pl. 14.
7) Brailsford, *o.c.*, pp. 16-17.
8) E.g. items from the Scottish Traprain Law and Roman Esquiline treasures (see p. 13, nn. 3-4).

directly with a specific cult, appears in its embossed reliefs. Certainly these vessels, the only distinguished 'minor' works of art that the London temple has produced, were Mediterranean imports; and it might seem natural to assign their importation to the wealthy, late second-century Mithraists who introduced from abroad the mid-imperial marble sculptures (p. 1). They must have been comparatively costly objects, not, apparently, in keeping with the shabby structure of the shrine as restored during the fourth century after its original stone colonnades had been removed, probably earlier in the same century [1]); and, as has already been pointed out (p. 9), the elegant plasticity of the casket's craftsmanship might be thought indicative of second-century work. But its closest stylistic affinities are, as we have also seen (pp. 9-11), with late-antique mosaic pavements; and that is the main consideration which must be set against the difficulty, on social and economic grounds, of connecting such fine vessels of precious metal with the latest phases of the temple's history and which appears to weight the balance in favour of detecting in them the products of a late third—, or early fourth—, century, possibly east-Mediterranean, workshop (cf. p. 15).

If the above dating of it is correct, the casket illustrates that persistence of good craftsmanship in contemporary silver work, in pagan as well as in Christian circles, to which the Mildenhall, [2]) Traprain Law [3]), Esquiline [4]), and other late Roman silver treasures, and such isolated pieces as the Parabiago patera, now at Milan [5]), bear striking witness; and given the means to pay for them, or the devotees able and willing to present them, the Walbrook silver

---

1) *JRS*, XLV, 1955, p. 138.
2) See p. 12, n. 1.
3) A. O. Curle, *The Treasure of Traprain: a Scottish Hoard of Roman Silver Plate*, 1923.
4) O. M. Dalton, *Catalogue of Early Christian Antiquities in the British Museum*, 1901, pp. 61-77, nos. 304-45, pls. 13-20.
5) Published by A. Levi in *La patera d'argento di Parabiago* (R. Istituto d'Archeologia e Storia dell'Arte; Opere d'Arte V), 1935, and by E. Strong in *The Burlington Magazine*, LXXII, 1938, upper fig. on p. 92 and p. 96, both of whom, it is interesting to note, attributed the piece to the second century. Its correct, fourth-century date was first perceived by A. Alföldi, *Die Kontorniaten*, 1942-3, pl. 71, fig. 1 and pp. 69-70.

vessels, with their 'neutral' reliefs and modest dimensions, could have been smuggled unobtrusively into the reconditioned temple, if they did not arrive at Walbrook, as seems, perhaps, more likely, a relatively short time before the dismantling of the shrine's colonnades in the earlier fourth century (pp. 1,13).

Assuming that the casket with its strainer served a ritual purpose (pp. 8-9), it is probable that its animal groups and hunting episodes carried a generally symbolic meaning for those who used it, as alluding, as has been already said (pp. 11-12), partly to the teeming life of paradise and partly to the hunting down of evil by divine power. The man drawn from the cage as a human bait might possibly suggest a ritual death and resurrection [1]). Furthermore, these designs may even have conveyed to the initiated a specifically Mithraic connotation, since Mithras figures in art as a mounted hunter, pursuing and slaying the forces of wickedness and death, as on the obverse of a two-sided sculptured slab from Dieburg [2]), on the reverse of a similar slab from Rückingen [3]), in one of the small scenes that frame the great bull-slaying relief from Osterburken [4]), and in a couple of mural paintings from the Dura-Europos

---

1) For a "grave" probably designed for such a ritual "death", see I. A. Richmond and J. P. Gillam, *The Temple of Mithras at Carrawburgh*, 1951, pp. 19-20, pl. 6. There seems to have been a similar "grave" in one of the rooms adjacent to the Mithraeum under the Church of Santa Prisca on the Aventine in Rome (M. J. Vermaseren and C. C. van Essen, *The Excavations under the Church of Santa Prisca at Rome*, Leiden (Brill) in print).

2) F. Behn, *Das Mithrasheiligtum zu Dieburg*, 1928, pp. 11-16, pl. 1. Mithras is accompanied by three hunting dogs, but his prey does not appear.

3) H. Birkner, *Denkmäler des Mithraskultes vom Kastell Rückingen* in *Germania*, XXX, 1952, pp. 349-62, pl. 24; M. J. Vermaseren, *Corpus Inscriptionum et Monumentorum Religionis Mithriacae*, II, 1960, pp. 80-2, no. 1137, fig. 297.

4) Cumont, *MMM*, II, 1896, p. 350, no. 246, pl. 6: in the second scene from the bottom on the right-hand side Mithras is shooting with bow and arrow, but his quarry is not shown. Mithras appears as a rider, but not necessarily as a hunter, on imperial-age coins of Trebizond in Pontus (*ibid.*, pp. 189-91, no. 3 bis, a-c, figs. 13-16) and on a relief from Neuenheim, where he gallops through a forest accompanied by a lion and a snake (*ibid.*, p. 424, no. 310, fig. 357; H. Schoppa, *Die Kunst der Römerzeit in Gallien, Germanien und Britannien*, 1957, pl. 88; Vermaseren, *o.c.*, II, 1960, p. 117, no. 1289, fig. 338). In the second and fifth small scenes from the right on the border along the top of the great Mithras Tauroctonos slab from Neuenheim, Mithras is shown as an archer, but is not mounted (Cumont, *MMM*, II, 1896, p. 346, no. 245c, pl. 5; Vermaseren, *o.c.*, II, 1960, pp. 114-6, no. 1283, fig. 337).

Mithraeum [1]). There can, again, be little doubt that Mithras the hunter is depicted in the unmounted figure that wears a Phrygian cap, has crosses and stars embroidered on the skirt of his tunic, and holds a bow, worked *en barbotine* on one side of a 'Castor' beaker from Verulamium [2]).

As to where the casket was manufactured, no conclusive internal criteria are forthcoming from the piece itself. We know virtually nothing of local styles in silver ware under the later Empire, if, indeed, such styles existed; nor have we any notion of the extent to which silver workers may have travelled from centre to centre in the service of their patrons. There is not a piece in the Mildenhall treasure, for instance, of which we can do more than guess the origin, basing our guesses on nothing more compelling than argument from general probabilities [3]). Similarly, all that we can say about the Walbrook casket is that the provenances and affinities (in the case of Piazza Armerina) of the late mosaics, with which we have related its decoration, are eastern; and that it is at least a possibility that its maker worked in, or hailed from, one of the eastern provinces. As to the strainer, we can, again, only say that it is likely to be of Mediterranean, rather than of northern or western provincial, origin.

1) Ed. M. C. Rostovtzeff, F. E. Brown, and C. B. Welles, *The Excavations at Dura-Europos: Preliminary Report of the Seventh and Eighth Seasons of Work, 1933-4 and 1934-5* 1939, pls. 14-15; Vermaseren, *o.c.*, I, 1956, pp. 68-9, no. 52, fig. 24. A snake, regarded here, as in the bull-slaying scene, as a symbol of life through death, accompanies the god, who is charging six wild animals. *Cf.* p. 14 n. 4 and the rearing snakes on the wall of the Walbrook casket, which seem to be assisting the hunters against the wild creatures (p. 5).

Hunting scenes also appear on fragments of an epistyle (now in the Salzburg Museum) from the Mithraic sanctuary found near Schloss Moosham in Unternberg i. Lungau (*Salzburger Museum Carolino Augusteum: Jahresschrift*, 1956, pp. 237-8, pl. 13).

2) *Archaeologia*, XC, 1944, pp. 121-2, fig. 20, no. 1; Toynbee, *o.c.*, p. 190, no. 157, pl. 190.

3) Brailsford, *o.c.*, p. 23.

PLATE I

The Lid.

PLATE II

Detail of the Lid.

PLATE III

Detail of the Lid.

PLATE IV

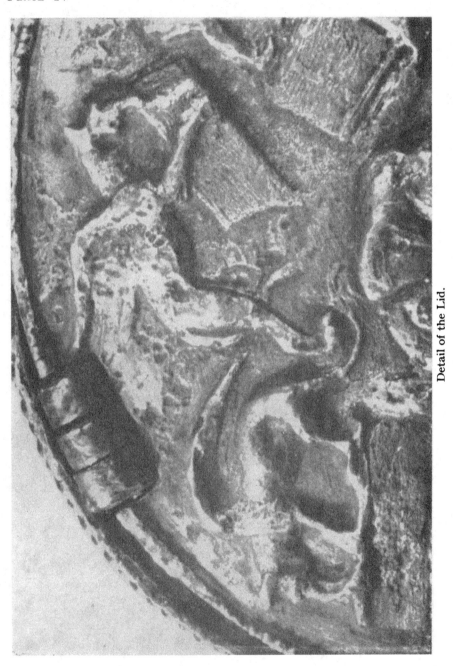

Detail of the Lid.

PLATE V

Detail of the Wall.

PLATE VI

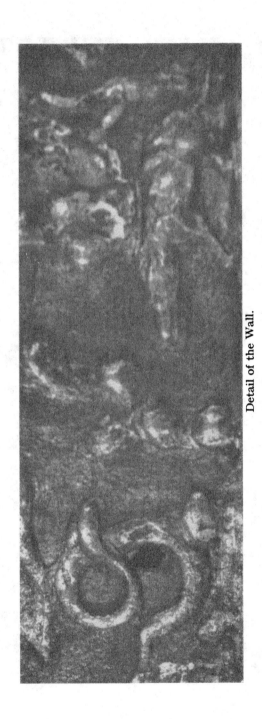

Detail of the Wall.

PLATE VII

Detail of the Wall.

Rolled-out View

PLATE VIII

View of the Wall.

PLATE IX

Detail of the Wall.

PLATE X

The Base of the Casket.

PLATE XI

The Strainer.

PLATE XII

The Stráže Strainer.

PLATE XIII

The Bottom of the Strainer.

PLATE XIV

Detail of the Lid.

PLATE XV

Detail of the Great Corridor Mosaic in the Villa near Piazza Armerina, Sicily.

Printed in the United States
By Bookmasters